HOPE
FOR A HELPLESS
PLANET

HOPE FOR A HELPLESS PLANET

CHRIS HOLLAND

Pacific Press®
Publishing Association

Nampa, Idaho | Oshawa, Ontario, Canada
www.pacificpress.com

Cover design by Gerald Lee Monks
Cover design resources from iStockphoto.com
Inside design by Kristin Hansen-Mellish

Copyright © 2016 by Pacific Press® Publishing Association
Printed in the United States of America
All rights reserved

Scriptures are taken from the New King James Version®. Copyright © 1982 by Thomas Nelson. Used by permission. All rights reserved.

You can obtain additional copies of this book by calling toll-free 1-800-765-6955 or by visiting http://www.adventistbookcenter.com.

ISBN 978-0-8163-6209-7

July 2016

Dedication

I dedicate this, my first book, to my mom, who first taught me what faithful, relentless love for the prodigal looks like.

And to the memory of my Grandma Bendit, who passed away during the production of this book. She lived a life of dedication and commitment to God and her family. Because of the hope we have in Jesus' return, we will see her again.

Contents

Introduction

This earth and it's inhabitants is the only planet in the universe that rebelled against the government of God. That rebellion has led this earth on an out of control spiral for more than six millennia. The newspaper, blogs, Twitter, and television demonstrate the helplessness of our planet. This spiral has led many to wonder: Is there anything to hope for? The Bible shows us that there is hope for today and our future. That hope comes in a promise given almost two thousand years ago. In the next few chapters, I invite you on a journey to find hope in the midst of the chaos of the world today.

The Promise

"Do not let your heart be troubled."
—*John 14:1*

Ernest Shackleton was born in Ireland, the son of a doctor. Ernest was an avid reader and, as a result of that reading, developed a strong sense of adventure. While his father had high aspirations of his son becoming a doctor, Ernest had other ideas. His desire to explore led him to join the merchant navy and by the young age of twenty-four he became a master mariner. Shackleton desired to explore the poles of the earth, especially the South Pole. In 1902, Shackleton, along with fellow explorer Robert Falcon Scott set a record for going the furthest south and closest to the south pole. Shackleton went on several other explorations to the south, but the most famous is the Trans-Antarctic expedition of 1914. The goal was to transverse the Antarctic. The adventure required two crews, one to make the journey, the other to place the supplies for a successful journey. Shackleton set out on that fantastic journey in the ship, *Endurance*.

As the *Endurance* drew nearer and nearer to Antarctic, the ship was surrounded and eventually totally blocked in by ice. They hoped to weather the danger and wait it out until the spring thaw then continue their journey. However, the ice pressed in harder and harder on the *Endurance* until it eventually breached the hull. Shackleton and his crew were forced to abandon ship. The *Endurance* sank. For two months the party camped on ice floes hoping that they would drift toward Paulet Island. Paulet Island would provide refuge and safety along a commonly used shipping route. However those plans were dashed. The ice floe they were on began to break up and the party was forced into their lifeboats and they eventually found themselves on Elephant Island. Because it was remote and away from any shipping routes, Shackleton knew that if his crew stayed on Elephant Island, there would be no rescue and certain death. He knew that he needed to take a risk and do something out of the ordinary to save his men. He decided he would take five men with him and set sail for South Georgia Island in a small boat hoping to get the help they needed. Leaving twenty-two men behind, he left them with a promise that he would return to take them home. In a circumstance of complete hopelessness, Shackleton promised that he would return.

* * * * *

Hopelessness. We live in a world that seems to offer very little in the way of hope. We look around the world today and see that it seems to be falling apart: wars and uprisings, unsolved hunger and famine, a teetering economy that could implode, and the general polarization of society. What is a person to do?

This hopelessness and despair reminds me of an event in the Bible when the apostle John shares the experience of the disciples just before Jesus was arrested and eventually killed. The disciples had just spent their last meal with Jesus.

He was trying to prepare them for all that was soon to take place. In John 13:31–35 it is recorded,

> So, when he had gone out, Jesus said, "Now the Son of Man is glorified, and God is glorified in Him. If God is glorified in Him, God will also glorify Him in Himself, and glorify Him immediately. Little children, I shall be with you a little while longer. You will seek Me; and as I said to the Jews, 'Where I am going, you cannot come,' so now I say to you. A new commandment I give to you, that you love one another; as I have loved you, that you also love one another. By this all will know that you are My disciples, if you have love for one another."

This teaching left His disciples confused, where was their master going? Why was He going to leave? Why couldn't they go with him? Then Peter, in his very aggressive style engaged Jesus further in verses 36–38, "Simon Peter said to Him, 'Lord, where are You going?' Jesus answered him, 'Where I am going you cannot follow Me now, but you shall follow Me afterward.' Peter said to Him, 'Lord, why can I not follow You now? I will lay down my life for Your sake.' Jesus answered him, 'Will you lay down your life for My sake? Most assuredly, I say to you, the rooster shall not crow till you have denied Me three times.' "

Can you imagine what a crushing blow this was for Peter to hear? Jesus was Peter's teacher, he had spent three and a half years with Him. He desired to be as close to Jesus as possible. He was a part of Jesus' inner circle and now Jesus told him that he would betray his beloved teacher. On that night when Jesus was trying to prepare them for the coming events, they were confused and didn't understand. What could Jesus do? He shared words of comfort; words that would bring security in the midst of uncertainty. Listen to Jesus, "Let not your heart be troubled; you believe in God, believe also in Me. In My Father's house are many mansions; if it were not so, I would have told you. I go to prepare a place for you. And if I go and prepare a place for you, I will come again and receive you to Myself; that where I am, there you may be also. And where I go you know, and the way you know" (John 14:1–4).

Can you hear the loving voice of Jesus trying to bring comfort to Peter and the rest of the disciples? The disciples, who were distraught over Jesus' prediction of His death, and Peter, who was troubled by his predicted denial, are given hope. What is the hope that Jesus provides? Hope in the Second Coming. Hope that even though Jesus was going to leave them, He would come back for them. The second coming of Jesus is the hope of every person on this earth. The second coming of Jesus can be your hope today. Through all types of turmoil and through every challenge faced in life, the hope for this helpless planet is the return of Jesus Christ.

The apostle Paul had these words to say in Titus 2:11–14, "For the grace of God that brings salvation has appeared to all men, teaching us that, denying ungodliness and worldly lusts, we should live soberly, righteously, and godly in the present age, looking for the blessed hope and glorious appearing of our great God and Savior Jesus Christ, who gave Himself for us, that He might redeem us from every lawless deed and purify for Himself His own special people, zealous for good works." Notice that Paul refers to the Second Coming as the blessed hope.

Why does the Second Coming give us hope?

Well, let's first ask, what is hope?

According to *Merriam-Webster's Dictionary, hope* is defined as "the feeling of wanting something to happen and thinking that it could happen."

Jesus wants to assure us that things will turn out for the best. How so?

John 3:16 contains that answer, a verse that is well known, "For God so loved the world that He gave His only begotten Son, that whoever believes in Him should not perish but have everlasting life." Whoever believes will have everlasting life, but reading the next verse brings even more hope and comfort. Continuing on to verse 17, "For God did not send His Son into the world to condemn the world, but that the world through Him might be saved."

Notice that Jesus was sent to save the world not condemn it. Too often Christianity presents the idea that God is out there somewhere with a watchful eye, waiting for you to make the wrong move and then zap! He's got you. But no, Jesus hasn't come with the intention of condemning people, He did not come to destroy people. Jesus came to save you and He is coming again to take you home with Him.

Do you remember those words that Jesus spoke in John 14? "Let not your hearts be troubled." There may be great disappointment in your life; you may be facing unexpected challenges. Maybe you're fighting cancer, maybe you're going through a divorce or maybe life seems to be overwhelming you from all sides. Jesus draws near and says, "Let not your hearts be troubled" Why? Because Jesus says "you believe in God, believe also in Him." Then Jesus promises that in heaven there are many mansions or some of the modern versions of the Bible translate it rooms. The promise here is not based on materialistic riches but on proximity. *Proximity to Jesus.*

Jesus promises that He has gone to heaven to prepare a place for you. Not just a general you, but for you personally. In fact, when you repeat the verse, why not use the word *me*. Jesus has gone to prepare a place for me and for you. That is where He lives, you may also live there. This was the whole purpose of Jesus' first coming. He would pave the way for us to be reunited with Him forever. But we all face a huge problem. Romans 6:23 states, "For the wages of sin is death" and then Romans 3:23 further emphasizes that problem, "for all have sinned and fall short of the glory of God." This does not give us good prospects for the future. The wages of sin is death and all have sinned. Our destiny seems bleak. But you know, I didn't quote the latter part of Romans 6:23, it goes on to say, "but the gift of God is eternal life in Christ Jesus our Lord." This is why Jesus is coming again, to give us the fulfillment of His promise of eternal life. This is why Jesus can say in John 14, "and if I go and prepare a place, I will come again." Do you hear those words? I will come again.

Now, let me share with you some insight on those words that bring an even greater depth of hope. As we read, "I will come again," we know that in the English language that phrase is in the future tense. However, in the original language it was not. As you may already know, the New Testament of the Bible was originally written in Greek. And in Greek, it is actually written in the present tense. You see, when John wrote these words he employed a grammatical technique called the futuristic present. What does that mean? An author would write something in the present tense but have a future meaning to convey that the event was so sure, was so definite, that it was to be written as if it was already happening or had happened. John lays out the assurance that Jesus is coming again. And remember He is coming for you, He is coming for me—in fact He's prepared a place for you, He's prepared a place for me. What does this all mean?

Well friend, Jesus loves you so much that He wants to spend eternity with you, but the question is, do you want to spend eternity with Him? It's a choice He freely gives to you. But what will you decide? Jesus wants you there.

But today many people have discounted the words of the Bible. Some poke fun at this Book, and numerous people have discounted the promises of His second coming found throughout the Bible. But this shouldn't surprise us. Peter warned us almost two thousand years ago, in his second letter, in chapter three, verses three and four, "knowing this first: that scoffers will come in the last days, walking according to their own lusts, and saying, 'Where is the promise of His coming? For since the fathers fell asleep, all things continue as they were from the beginning of creation.' " A scoffer is someone who ridicules things and doesn't believe. Peter warns that there will be people who will ridicule those who believe in the second coming of Jesus. They will say that the earth has always existed and it will continue to exist without any interruption. They will say, "Jesus isn't coming, you're silly to believe in such fairy tales."

But friends by just reading or listening to the news, we realize the turmoil of this earth. Paul wrote these words in Romans 8:20–22, "For the creation was subjected to futility, not willingly, but because of Him who subjected it in hope; because the creation itself also will be delivered from the bondage of corruption into the glorious liberty of the children of God. For we know that the whole creation groans and labors with birth pangs together until now." The whole earth itself was subject to the curse of sin and all the upheaval in the world we see is the earth groaning to be freed by the coming of Jesus. Everything happening around us points to Jesus' soon return. But wait, don't those scoffers have a point? After all, it has been two thousand years from the time when Jesus gave that promise. But notice again what Peter says in 2 Peter 3:8, 9, "But, beloved, do not forget this one thing, that with the Lord one day is as a thousand years, and a thousand years as one day. The Lord is not slack concerning His promise, as some count slackness, but is longsuffering toward us, not willing that any should perish but that all should come to repentance."

For God, time is irrelevant. He is not confined by our rendering of time. But more importantly, the Bible says that Jesus isn't slack or relaxed concerning the promise of His return. But He is longsuffering. A very special word that conveys an extraordinary patience. Why has He been so patient and hasn't returned? Because He doesn't want any to perish, Jesus came to this earth so that no one had to die eternally and that all would come to repentance and be saved.

* * * * *

Ernest Shackleton and his five men left Elephant Island for South Georgia.

Aware of the great difficulties they would face on their eighteen hundred nautical-mile journey, Shackleton packed only four weeks of supplies. He knew the crew wouldn't survive any longer than that. Through treacherous seas and a storm that produced winds strong enough to sink a five-hundred-ton ship, that crew finally made it to South Georgia Island. Once arriving on the shores of the island,

Shackleton and part of his crew still had to hike more than thirty miles to get to the whaling station—the only inhabited part of the island. After finally arriving at the whaling station, Shackleton gathered another crew for the rescue mission. Now came the most daunting task—returning to Elephant Island for that promised rescue. Four months after leaving Elephant Island, Shackleton returned to save his men. At times, some of those men may have wondered if he was really returning. They may have wondered if he would keep his promise. However, Shackleton's entire crew was saved. Even though they lost the ship *Endurance*, each one of them endured to the end. Shackleton delivered on his promise and he was proclaimed a hero.

Jesus has made a promise. He has promised that He is coming again. He is coming to take His children home. That home, which is pictured in Revelation 21:1–5,

> Now I saw a new heaven and a new earth, for the first heaven and the first earth had passed away. Also there was no more sea. Then I, John, saw the holy city, New Jerusalem, coming down out of heaven from God, prepared as a bride adorned for her husband. And I heard a loud voice from heaven saying, "Behold, the tabernacle of God is with men, and He will dwell with them, and they shall be His people. God Himself will be with them and be their God. And God will wipe away every tear from their eyes; there shall be no more death, nor sorrow, nor crying. There shall be no more pain, for the former things have passed away." Then He who sat on the throne said, "Behold, I make all things new." And He said to me, "Write, for these words are true and faithful."

No more suffering, no more pain—all things new. Everything working the way that it was originally intended to be—perfect harmony, perfect peace. This is what Jesus wants for you and for me. It is what He promised. Today, do you want to ask Jesus into your heart and make a decision to follow Him fully? Jesus desires to take you home. He says these words as recorded in Revelation 3:20, "Behold, I stand at the door and knock." Jesus knocks today, will you let Him in?

The apostle Paul also gives us comfort and hope in describing the day Jesus returns in his first letter to the Thessalonians, chapter four, verses fifteen through eighteen,

> For this we say to you by the word of the Lord, that we who are alive and remain until the coming of the Lord will by no means precede those who are asleep. For the Lord Himself will descend from heaven with a shout, with the voice of an archangel, and with the trumpet of God. And the dead in Christ will rise first. Then we who are alive and remain shall be caught up together with them in the clouds to meet the Lord in the air. And thus we shall always be with the Lord. Therefore comfort one another with these words.

We shall always be with the Lord. No wonder that we are to comfort one another with these words!

Whatever your situation may be, Jesus wants to encourage you—He wants to give you hope. Are you facing an illness? Jesus says, "Don't let your heart be troubled." Are you facing marital challenges? Jesus wants to give you assurance. Are you facing a problem in the work place? Jesus reaches out to encourage you. Whatever you face today, on this hopeless and helpless planet Jesus gives you hope.

Today, I invite you to cling to the hope of Jesus' soon return. Today is your opportunity to invite Him into your heart and commit yourself to Him. Jesus invites you today, in His words in Matthew 11:28, 29, "Come to Me, all you who labor and are heavy laden, and I will give you rest. Take My yoke upon you and learn from Me, for I am gentle and lowly in heart, and you will find rest for your souls."

Signs of Hope—Part 1

*"Tell us, when will these things be? And what will be the
sign of Your coming, and of the end of the age?"*
—Matthew 24:3

In the twilight hours of April 14, 1912, the RMS *Titanic*
sped through the icy waters of the Atlantic. At the last
moment, an iceberg was spotted. The Titanic maneuvered
to avoid that iceberg, but it tore a gash in the side of the
magnificent ship. Almost three hours later the ship sank and
more than fifteen hundred crew and passengers perished in
the frigid waters. Could it be that this one-hundred-year-old
story has a lesson for us today? Could it be that this story
sheds light on a teaching of Jesus from almost two thousand
years ago?

In 1908 White Star Line contracted to have Olympic-class
vessels built. White Star was trying to stay on the cutting
edge by building the largest cruise ships in the industry.
Those ships would eventually be known as the *Olympic* and
the *Titanic*. Titanic boasted a length of almost one thousand
feet, a width of almost one hundred feet and a height of
more than one hundred feet. It was the largest ship at that
time. This enormous boat was a luxurious liner. Even the
third class passenger facilities were lavish compared to other
vessels. The *Titanic* and *Olympic* were deemed the largest

and finest steamers in the world. Many experts of the day believed them to be unsinkable. However, as we know today, the *Titanic* was not the unsinkable ship she was thought to be.

On April 10, 1912, the fateful journey of the *Titanic* began. In the days leading up to the disaster, the *Titanic* received several warning messages of drifting ice in the area. Under normal operating procedures of the times, the *Titanic* continued cruising at full speed. The ship simply placed a lookout to watch for any imminent danger. Unfortunately, the spotter saw the iceberg too late, and the *Titanic* sank after striking the iceberg, killing more than fifteen hundred people. It is a tragedy of historic proportions. Today, some of the artifacts from this terrible disaster are on display at the Maritime Museum of the Atlantic in Halifax, Nova Scotia.

The *Titanic* received many warnings but ignored them. That choice cost many lives. Is it possible that we are living at a time when we have received many warnings, yet, we have ignored them? Is it possible that despite the numerous warnings, we, like the *Titanic* are simply cruising through life at full speed?

Almost two thousand years ago Jesus gave warning signs. He presented signs of His second coming. Those signs were given, so that we might know that it was nearing.

As Jesus was concluding His ministry, just before He was arrested and ultimately killed, He met with His disciples. Matthew 24 records Jesus' description of how the temple in Jerusalem would be destroyed. The disciples were troubled by this prospect. So His disciples came to Him asking questions, beginning in verse 1,

Then Jesus went out and departed from the temple,

and His disciples came up to show Him the buildings of the temple. And Jesus said to them, "Do you not see all these things? Assuredly, I say to you, not one stone shall be left here upon another, that shall not be thrown down."

Now as He sat on the Mount of Olives, the disciples came to Him privately, saying, "Tell us, when will these things be? And what will be the sign of Your coming, and of the end of the age?"

The disciples asked Jesus two questions—when would the temple be destroyed and what was the sign of His second coming? The disciples thought that those two events were one in the same. However, they were and are distinct from one another. Jesus, as He sat on the Mount of Olives, overlooking Jerusalem, painted a vivid picture of a time when Jerusalem would be destroyed. He pointed forward to 70 A.D. when the Roman armies, led by General Titus, would come and not leave one stone upon another. The disciples thought for sure that such a catastrophic event must precede the Lord's return, but they misunderstood. Frankly, they may not have been able to endure the true nature of all of the events to come. So as Jesus answered He blended His answer so as not to overwhelm His disciples. They were unprepared for a full disclosure of future events. After Jesus' death, burial, resurrection, and ascension, the disciples continued to study the words of Jesus and with the guidance of the promised Holy Spirit they gained a more complete understanding. Today, like those early disciples, we are studying the words of Jesus to discover what words of warning He has for us.

When reading a book or watching a movie, the final

chapter of the book or the final minutes of that movie is often the climax. In that final chapter or minutes, tensions are resolved and everything that book or movie was driving towards is brought to a conclusion. The Bible is no different. The Bible is replete with warnings to God's people and in the last chapter and verses the final warning is given that all other warnings point to. In Revelation 22:7, Jesus says, "Behold, I am coming quickly!" And then again in verse 12, "And behold, I am coming quickly, and My reward is with Me, to give to every one according to his work." And finally in verse 20, He says again, "Surely I am coming quickly." In the last chapter of the Bible with great urgency, Jesus tells us three times that He is coming quickly. In this chapter, we're studying specifically the warnings given in Matthew 24 that point directly to the nearness of His coming. These warnings are in reality encouragements to be steadfast in our faith and to cling more closely to Him.

As we begin this study, I want to share with you a key principle in understanding the timing of the Lord's return. In Matthew 24:36, Jesus is very clear, "But of that day and hour no one knows, not even the angels of heaven, but My Father only." Did you hear that? No one knows the exact time of the Lord's return. So if any pastor, preacher, or teacher begins sharing that they know the exact timing of the Lord's second coming—we can know that they are not operating according to biblical principles. Yet we ought to care about the nearness of Jesus' return because in verse 42, He goes on to say, "Watch therefore, for you do not know what hour your Lord is coming" and in verse 44, "Therefore you also be ready, for the Son of Man is coming at an hour you do not expect." In these verses, Jesus gives us two key principles that will enable us to be prepared for His return—watch and be ready. In chapter 24 He tells us what to watch for and gives us the signs of His soon return. Then in chapter 25 He tells us how to be ready through three parables. Those two principles of watch and be ready, prepare us for that day of glorious hope when Jesus will come and take us from this hopeless and helpless world.

What does it mean to watch? The original language gives the idea that this word is defined as being on the alert, being vigilant and having a zealous watchfulness. This watching is not just a casual glance, but an intent gaze. This type of watching pays attention to the details so as to not miss anything.

With Just over three minutes to play in the gold medal women's hockey matchup at the Sochi Olympics, the US women's team held a 2 to 0 lead over the Canadian team. However, in a shocking turn of events, the Canadian team tied the game with less than two minutes remaining and sent the match into overtime, where they won the gold medal. Imagine for just a moment that you had watched the entire game and in those closing three minutes you figured the game was over and left to pop a bag of microwave popcorn, or use the washroom, or gather your mail. In just those few minutes, you would have missed some of the most exciting moments of Olympic history.

When Jesus said watch, He didn't mean that we should stare up in the clouds all day long, but He intended for us to carefully observe what is going on in the world around us. Don't misunderstand what I am saying, we should dwell on heavenly things and fill our mind with heavenly thoughts— yet at the same time we need to be observant of the happenings on this earth and see the signs. We need to watch until the very end.

Mark 13 is a parallel chapter to Matthew 24. It shares the same event but from a different perspective. Notice Jesus' comment about watching in Mark 13:28, 29, "Now learn this parable from the fig tree: When its branch has already become tender, and puts forth leaves, you know that summer is near. So you also, when you see these things happening, know that it is near—at the doors!"

Jesus gave a simple illustration, when we see the buds on tree branches we know the change of season is at hand. After the harshness of winter, the breaking of tree buds tells us that the warmth of summer is on its way. In the same way, Jesus gave signs in Matthew 24 indicating that His return is soon, even though we do not know the day or the hour.

What are the signs of His return? As we study this chapter we will see that the signs of His return can be grouped into four categories: signs in the religious world, political world, natural world, and cultural world.

The signs in the religious world are recorded in Matthew 24:23, 24, "Then if anyone says to you, 'Look, here is the Christ!' or 'There!' do not believe it. For false christs and false prophets will rise and show great signs and wonders to deceive, if possible, even the elect."

There is the true Christ and there are true prophets, but Jesus says that there will be counterfeits. The challenge in many of these cases is that counterfeits are not always easy to recognize. In fact Revelation 16:14 says, "For they are spirits of demons, performing signs, which go out to the kings of the earth and of the whole world, to gather them to the battle of that great day of God Almighty." Satan works through them to perform signs, which deceive and confuse. So often error is not outright error, but it is truth mixed with error.

This is what makes counterfeits so dangerous—they are

often a lot of truth mixed with just a small amount of error. You never find a person who introduces himself or herself as a card-carrying member of the false prophets club, do you? No the error is often couched in truth.

When counterfeiters make bills, you don't see them counterfeiting thirteen-dollar bills, do you? Why not? Because they don't exist, of course. Counterfeiters will try to copy the genuine article.

In May 2000, the town of Walkerton, Ontario, seemed like any other small Ontario town. But suddenly many of the townspeople began getting sick. Little did they know, the town's water supply had been contaminated with the deadly E. coli bacteria—a silent killer that doesn't have a taste or smell. People drank the water because drinking water is good for you. But this, good-for-you drink had been contaminated with a poison. It was good and bad mixed, and the bad made people sick, in fact at least seven people died.

The devil often wraps error with enough truth to make it palatable. Knowing this, what can we use as a standard for truth? 2 Timothy 3:16, 17 says, "All Scripture is given by inspiration of God, and is profitable for doctrine, for reproof, for correction, for instruction in righteousness, that the man of God may be complete, thoroughly equipped for every good work."

Scripture is the litmus test. It will mark with distinction what is truth and what is error. It will make clear what is true and what is false.

Friend, I must tell you, beware of any teacher that steers you from the Bible. It is our only true guide. Too many today make decisions based on emotion and feeling, but God's Word gives us the foundation to help us make decisions based on principle.

The devil has packaged false teachers and false teachings in many different forms. Books, magazines, television programs, and movies featuring the occult are some of the most popular. These falsehoods have been aimed at our young people and teens seem to be the most fascinated by these teachings. Youth and young adults dominate the number of adherents to the occult and new members of cults.

False prophets and false christs will arise.

False teachers and leaders use their magnetic and mesmerizing personalities to deceive unsuspecting followers. There was Jim Jones who formed the People's Temple. He claimed to be the people's savior and in 1978 ordered a mass suicide—that day 909 people died by drinking cyanide-laced Kool-Aid.

In 1993 David Koresh made a stand against the US government in Waco, Texas. Koresh, who had a magnetic personality, drew a number of followers. He, too, claimed to be the messiah of Bible prophecy. On April 19, 1993, seventy-eight members of the Branch Davidians, including Koresh, perished when the US government entered their compound, and it caught on fire.

In Australia, AJ Miller claimed to be Jesus of Nazareth reincarnated. He claimed that in 2012 Brisbane, Melbourne and Sydney would be engulfed by the sea and would no longer exist—his predictions, of course, failed.

Apollo Quiboloy, founder of the Restorationist church in the Philippines, claims to be the appointed son of God.

False teachers will lead many astray.

Marshall Applewhite, whose piercing eyes have been seen in the many news magazines and television programs, was known as John Doe. He led the Heaven's Gate cult. He taught his followers that the famous Hale-Bopp comet was being trailed by a spacecraft that would receive them and take them to a place of bliss. Between March 22–26, 1997, thirty-nine individuals took their lives in the hope of finding bliss.

Friends, while these may seem easy to identify and easy to avoid, many people have been deceived. And while these are scattered instances, the Bible tells us that there will be a deception of a global nature that all who dwell on the earth will face.

Revelation 13:13, 14 predicts this about the end times, just before the return of Jesus, "He [the prophetic lamb-like beast that came out of the earth] performs great signs, so that he even makes fire come down from heaven on the earth in the sight of men. And he deceives those who dwell on the earth—by those signs which he was granted to do in the sight of the beast, telling those who dwell on the earth to make an image to the beast who was wounded by the sword and lived."

Do you see the common thread in the deceptions we read about in the Bible? There will be amazing and seemingly miraculous signs and wonders that lead many to be deceived. Friends, we cannot allow that which is exciting to dictate what is truth and error.

All these signs in the religious world should not discourage us. There is hope for this helpless planet. These signs point to the reality that Jesus is coming soon. The time to cling to Him is now.

But Jesus also said that there would be signs in the political world in Matthew 24:6, "And you will hear of wars and rumors of wars. See that you are not troubled; for all these things must come to pass, but the end is not yet. For nation will rise against nation, and kingdom against kingdom. And there will be famines, pestilences, and earthquakes in various places."

When you look back over the course of the twentieth century, what you find is that it was the bloodiest century of all in history. The twenty-first century brought 180 million deaths from war. In a society that many claim is getting better and better—reality would suggest otherwise. Jesus predicted a rise in war.

- In the first fourteen years of the twenty-first century there have been more than twenty-five wars and well over half-million casualties.
- Today there are fragile peace agreements. Despite the many political spins on peace, so many areas of the world teeter on the brink of war.
- Countries like Libya and Egypt have experienced major political upheavals, Syria is still in the midst of crisis, Iraq and Afghanistan are extremely unstable, and Ukraine has also developed into a political hot spot.

This should come as no surprise, 1 Thessalonians 5:3 reads, "For when they say, 'Peace and safety!' then sudden destruction comes upon them."

Friends, Jesus predicted these signs, we don't need to worry, we don't need to be overwhelmed, we need to trust.

The Word of God is our only guide in this chaos of hopelessness. Jesus is our hope when we feel helpless. All of these signs point to His soon return when He will bring an end to sin, suffering, death, and dying. Jesus gave even more signs of His return, which give us the assurance the His coming is soon. But I want to leave you with this assurance of Jesus.

Even in all the turmoil of this world Jesus has given these signs of hope.

In Joshua 1:9 the Bible says, "Have I not commanded you? Be strong and of good courage; do not be afraid, nor be dismayed, for the LORD your God is with you wherever you go."

Jesus will be with you, He won't leave you or forsake you, but He invites you today to come into relationship with Him.

Joshua had these words of encouragement for the people of Israel on edges of the promised land in Joshua 24:15, "Choose for yourselves this day whom you will serve. . . . But as for me and my house, we will serve the LORD." Heaven is our promised land.

A choice to enter into a relationship with Jesus gives us assurance and hope, not just for then but for today as well, Deuteronomy 31:6 assures us, "Be strong and of good courage, do not fear nor be afraid of them; for the LORD your God, He is the One who goes with you. He will not leave you nor forsake you."

His signs of hope can give us courage as we face the future of tomorrow and the struggles of today. Oh friend, Jesus is reaching out His hand of courage today; won't you give your heart and life to Him right now?

Signs of Hope—Part 2

"And this gospel of the kingdom will be preached in all the world as a witness to all the nations, and then the end will come."
—Matthew 24:14

I n 1962 David Bernays and Charles Sawyer were on a mountain expedition investigating the Cordillera Blanco mountain range in Peru. Along their journey, they decided to investigate Glacier 511. Their findings were absolutely frightening. They saw that an enormous piece of the rock bed had been compromised by the glacier and just the slightest disturbance would release an avalanche that would spell certain doom for the town of Yungay in the valley below. Equipped with this ominous warning, the men contacted the authorities and newspaper. Instead of being grateful for the warning, Bernays and Sawyer were thrown into jail and threatened because of the hysteria they might cause. They were told to recant their story or face lengthy prison sentences. The men were able to escape the country and the authorities were able to suppress the warnings. Everything went back to normal, and nothing happened for several years. However, on May 31, 1970, Bernays and Sawyer's worst fears became reality. An undersea earthquake, named the Ancash earthquake, tipped the scale at 7.9 on the

Richter scale. The short quake set off a devastating turn of events. The movement of the earth shook loose the damage to the rockbed of the mountain sending a colossal avalanche, which included a half-mile section of glacier down the mountain. There was so much debris that it buried the entire city of Yungay, instantly killing twenty thousand people. The authorities ignored the warning, and their complacency and suppression of the truth resulted in a tragedy.

We are right now living in a time of warning. Jesus warned us almost two thousand years ago that this world was coming to an end. He gave signs to watch for that we might know how soon He is coming. In Matthew 24 Jesus gave us signs of His return to give hope to this helpless planet. Jesus taught that there would be signs in the religious world, the political world, the natural world, and the cultural world.

In the last chapter we reviewed the signs we are seeing fulfilled in the religious world. We see a rise in false teachings and a general pulling away from biblical truth. We also studied the increasing political tensions and wars in our world, knowing that those signs point to the coming of Jesus, but there are even more signs in the world to consider.

There has been a dramatic rise in the potential for world destruction. The world's ability to destroy itself is sobering. Revelation 11:18 cautions, "The nations were angry, and Your wrath has come, . . . and should destroy those who destroy the earth." Humanity's technological advances have led to weapons that can destroy the earth.

Just think of the countries with the known capacity for nuclear weapons: the United States, Russia, United Kingdom, France, and Japan. They have enough nuclear weapons on hand to destroy the earth many times over. And countries such as India, Pakistan, North Korea, Israel, and

Iran are all suspected of being capable of producing some type of nuclear weapon as well.

Sydney J. Harris's portentous words are now a living reality, "We are poised on the brink of the most calamitous conflict that can be imagined—indeed, it cannot even be imagined."

William Ripley, a journalist who covered the affects of the atomic bomb broadcast these almost prophetic words as he stood in the midst of the aftermath of Hiroshima, "I am standing on the place where the end of the world began."

What hope is there for this helpless planet? Only the return of Jesus. He will bring all of this turmoil and suspicion to an end.

Two thousand years ago, Jesus shared today's prevailing modern mind-set when He spoke these words in Luke 21:26, "Men's hearts failing them from fear and the expectation of those things which are coming on the earth, for the powers of the heavens will be shaken." People wonder today, *What do these things mean for me? What does this mean for my family? Is there any meaning at all? What hope do I have for today? Is there any hope for tomorrow?*

Jesus also warned that there would be signs in the natural world in Matthew 24:7, "And there will be famines, pestilences, and earthquakes in various places."

The study of things happening on this earth shows an increasing intensity of natural disasters. The increasing frequency of tornados, earthquakes, hurricanes, floods, and fires point to this planet being in distress.

Sadly, famines are happening all over this earth. While we in the West are rarely plagued with famine, many of us will never forget the tragic pictures of Ethiopian children and youth who are emaciated and hungry.

The United Nations reports that over thirty-five nations experience food shortage. One-sixth of the world's population is undernourished. Ten thousand people per day (more than 3.5 million people each year) die of starvation.

In 2012 the Associated Press reported that 80 percent of the people living in the Sudanese conflict were eating only one meager meal per day.

But famine wasn't the only sign Jesus gave, He also said that there would be pestilences. What is a pestilence? A pestilence is a strange disease that afflicts human beings, crops, and the environment. In addition, a pestilence can be new diseases that spring up around the world. Just think of some of those new diseases that were unheard of in previous generations: Lyme disease, Marburg Virus, HIV, AIDS, mad cow disease, bird flu, and H1N1 just to name a few. Many medical experts believe that our current antibiotics will no longer be able to provide a defense against the strongest pathogens.

Diseases of the plant life have grown increasingly complex to deal with. The loss of soil has weakened plants' natural resistance to pests and disease. Resistance to pesticides and herbicides grow stronger, requiring more chemicals which will potentially cause further damage to the environment. Premature deaths caused by more than a million pounds of toxic pollutants released yearly into the atmosphere are on the rise.

In 1992, 1,700 scientists met together and wrote a document entitled, "A Warning to Humanity." They said the following, "Human beings and the natural world are on a collision course. Human activities inflict harsh and often irreversible damage on the environment and on critical resources. If not checked, many of our current practices put at serious risk the future that we wish for human society and the plant and animal kingdoms, and may so alter the living world that it will be unable to sustain life in the manner that we know. Fundamental changes are urgent if we are to avoid the collision our present course will bring about."

Did you hear those words? Human beings and the natural world are on a collision course. In almost prophetic language, these scientists confirm what Jesus predicted would be a sign of His soon return. They went on to say that soon, "The chance to avert the threats we now confront will be lost and the prospects for humanity immeasurably diminished."

While these signs can cause great fear and distress, Jesus warned that they would happen. All of these events should draw us nearer and nearer to Jesus and we must rely on Him in this time of trouble.

In Matthew 24:7, He also cautioned that we would see earthquakes in various places.

The US geological survey estimates that, worldwide, there are on average more than forty earthquakes per day. That is more than fourteen thousand per year. Luke 21:11 echoes the words of Jesus in Mathew 24 where it is recorded, "And there will be great earthquakes in various places, and famines and pestilences; and there will be fearful sights and great signs from heaven."

The total chaos in the natural world has led many to wonder what is going to happen to this planet of ours. Describing this state of uncertainty and anxiety, Luke 21:26 reveals, "Men's hearts failing them from fear and the expectation of those things which are coming on the earth, for the powers of the heavens will be shaken." Is there any hope for the future? Is there any hope for today? Our only hope is in Jesus Christ.

The natural world continues to experience all types of turmoil . Tsunamis seem to be on the rise, occurring in various places such as Japan, Indonesia, Sumatra, and Turkey. Many remember the tragic December 26 Indian Oceean tsunami in 2004 during which an estimated 230,000 people died. This tsunami was set off by a 9.1 magnitude earthquake under the ocean which produced the destructive waves.

Although in some parts of the world, the 2013 hurricane season was one of the least active in decades, hurricanes have in recent years been increasing in numbers and intensity. The 2005 Atlantic hurricane season, with the most named storms in history, culminated with Hurricane Katrina. The central Gulf States of the United States were pounded by this storm leaving behind more than 100 billion dollars in damage. It had a 250-billion-dollar economic impact.

Romans 8:22 reflects this by saying, "For we know that the whole creation groans and labors with birth pangs together until now." These natural phenomena are like the labor pains of a woman, growing in strength and revealing that something is about to happen. Jesus has told us that, the "something," is His soon coming.

Jesus also taught that there would be signs in the culture. In Matthew 24:37, 38, He says, "But as the days of Noah were, so also will the coming of the Son of Man be. For as in the days before the flood, they were eating and drinking, marrying and giving in marriage, until the day that Noah entered the ark."

In Noah's day, there was rampant moral decay in the land. Genesis 6:5, 6 tell us what it was like in Noah's day, "Then the Lord saw that the wickedness of man was great in the earth, and that every intent of the thoughts of his heart was only evil continually. And the Lord was sorry that He had made man on the earth, and He was grieved in His heart." Man had reached a point of such degradation that God was actually sorry He had made mankind. Mankind was wicked to the very core. Genesis 6 :11, 12 further emphasize, "The earth also was corrupt before God, and the earth was filled with violence. So God looked upon the earth, and indeed it was corrupt; for all flesh had corrupted their way on the earth."

Corruption, evil, and wickedness were the words used to describe the time of Noah. Jesus said that it would be the same way on the earth just prior to His coming. Over the last several decades some of the greatest areas of moral decay in society have been the break-up of the family unit, and complacent attitudes toward spiritual things and moral living. During the last twenty-five years, the birth of babies to unwed mothers has increased almost threefold in Canada. And, depending on what part of the world you are in, 50 to 75 percent of all marriages end in divorce.

Worldwide crime and violence are on the rise in intensity and in numbers. Author Scott Christiansen speaks of the problem of densification—or the urbanization of society. As humanity moves closer into urban centers, it places more of the population in a smaller area. This densification has led to many problems, but one of the greatest is an increase of crime and violence.

The World Report on violence and health states, "Each year, more than 1.6 million people worldwide lose their lives to violence. . . . Many more are injured. . . . Violence is among the leading cause of death for people aged 15–44 accounting for 14% of deaths among males and 7% among females."

Jesus warned, "And because lawlessness will abound, the

41

love of many will grow cold." This lawlessness and violence in society has many contributing factors, but, no doubt, many experts will point to the increase of violence in the media as a major factor. The statistics are astounding—on average children watch three hours of television per day. By age twelve, through media, they've witnessed fourteen thousand murders. In addition there has been a large increase in the allowable foul language and sexual content in the media. It is no wonder that there is an increased moral decay.

Economic uncertainty is another sign in the world of society. James 5:1–3 sums up our situation well, "Come now, you rich, weep and howl for your miseries that are coming upon you! Your riches are corrupted, and your garments are moth-eaten. Your gold and silver are corroded, and their corrosion will be a witness against you and will eat your flesh like fire. You have heaped up treasure in the last days."

The banking crisis and collapse of major financial institutions brings to the forefront the greed that exists in our day. As one area in our world crumbles it often has a domino effect on other areas as well, creating a more catastrophic situation.

The uncertainty is real. The signs that Jesus gave almost two thousand years ago are being fulfilled with increasing intensity each day. We can see the signs in the religious world being fulfilled, the signs in the political world are all there, the natural world is in turmoil, and society is in total decay.

The signs point to the imminent return of Christ.

However, one of the most powerful signs of the return of Jesus is found in Matthew 24:14, "And this gospel of the kingdom will be preached in all the world as a witness to all the nations, and then the end will come." The gospel going to the entire world is one of the most definitive signs that Jesus is coming soon.

All around the world, people are more receptive to the gospel than ever before. Radio, television, and the Internet have opened territories that couldn't be entered just a few years ago. Today you can see that God is on the move. Thousands are being baptized each day. While there is a tremendous amount of work still to do, things are happening.

Some friends of mine led out in Bible prophecy lectures that took place in Angola, where more than eight thousand people were baptized. Other friends have been involved in outreach in India where over the course of ten years twenty thousand people have become baptized followers of Jesus. Even in the Western world, where society has become disinterested in the church, places such as New York and Chicago have seen explosive growth as the gospel is shared. God is on the move. His coming is very near.

Are you watching? Will you be ready?

It could be that the signs of the times that Jesus predicted that would happen globally are happening to you in a personal way. Maybe in your life, right now you are searching for truth. Maybe you wonder if there is any truth. Maybe you have found it difficult to believe in the God you have heard about. You owe it to yourself to come to the Bible and discover its truths. You can learn for yourself, first hand, the truth about a loving God and His plan to give you an abundant life, both now and eternally.

Maybe you are experiencing political tension and war in your family. I'm not talking about differences in political parties but the wars and clashing of ideals that families experience, particularly between parents and children. Where the various parties argue for their particular agendas and words are used like knives to cut and sometimes kill the ones we should love and care about the most. Do others see our families as being "perfect" yet within the walls of our homes, there is violence, abuse, neglect? God has something so much better in store for you. In a prophecy describing the days before Jesus returns, Malachi 4:5, 6 indicates that there will be a call for people to repent and that the heart of the fathers will be turned toward the children and the heart of the children to their fathers. Do want that for your family? Jesus promises that He can begin that work in your family today.

Maybe you see signs in your life from the natural world. Maybe you are going through something right now that is out of your control. Suffering from an illness or physical hunger, maybe you feel like there is a hurricane over your head and it is leaving untold physical and mental damage in its path. Jesus invites you to look to Him who can say to the storms of your life, "Peace, be still."

The moral decay of society is prevalent because of what is happening in the lives of individuals. Perhaps in one form or another you have witnessed acts of violence and crime; or maybe you have succumbed to societal pressures to do what feels right only to find out that it doesn't always end up right; if your activities have led you in circles or driven you to despair I invite you to accept the invitation of Jesus to look unto Him who is the Author and Finisher of our faith—the One who promises to give you a future and a hope.

You could be experiencing economic uncertainty in your life today, struggling just to make ends meet. Jesus again has the answer by asking us today to seek Him first and in 1 Peter 5:7 He invites you to "cast all your care upon Him for He cares for you."

In Matthew 24 the last sign that Jesus talks about is the gospel going to the entire world. Today, the gospel has come to you personally. Today you have seen the signs in world around you, you have seen the signs in your own life, and you have the opportunity to heed these warnings of Jesus.

Maybe you've been discouraged. Maybe you have slipped in your Christian walk. Maybe you've never engaged in a personal walk with Jesus. Why not take the hand of Jesus and be encouraged to watch and be ready today?

Maybe you're a faithful Christian and needed this encouragement to stay on the course.

Friends, no matter where you are or who you are, Jesus desires that we would watch and be ready.

Are you watching? The signs are being fulfilled. Won't you commit or recommit yourself to follow Jesus all the way, daily watching for His return?

The Return

"Behold, this is our God;
We have waited for Him, and He will save us.
This is the Lord,
We have waited for Him;
We will be glad and rejoice in His salvation."
—Isaiah 25:9

The humpback whale is one of the most majestic creatures on the earth. It is massive in size and amazing in its beauty. It is almost unimaginable that an animal that is sixteen meters long, weighing more than thirty tons can breach the water fully in display of its magnificent power. This mammal has a heart that weighs more than four hundred pounds, and during the feeding season, it eats more than two tons of plankton, krill, and other small fish every day. You can find whale watching tours all over the world. The north, east, and west coasts of Canada offer ample opportunity to see these grand creatures. On December 3, 2012, Captain Jerry Smyth, of Aquaventures Dive Center in Baltimore West Cork, Ireland, led a group of people on tour to see this king of the sea. They were aboard the *Wave Chieftain* pursuing a humpback whale. As the boat stopped, all the people were directed to look to the starboard side of the ship. They watched for the footprint left by the whale, and waited for the whale to surface. But then, in his now-famous picture, photographer Simon Duggan captured a humpback whale breaching—but everyone on the *Wave Chieftain* had their backs to the action. They were in the right place—but they looked the wrong way.

Friends, as we watch for Jesus' soon return, are we watching in the right direction? Do we know how Jesus will return? Or are we looking in all the wrong places?

Throughout history, each culture had a quest for immortality. In ancient Egypt, the pyramids were built to memorialize the pharaoh's pursuit of immortality. The ancient Babylonians sought after immortality, the Romans sought for immortality. The Incas and Mayans and their great pyramids were building quests for immortality. This shouldn't come as a surprise to any of us for the Bible says in Ecclesiastes 3:11, "Also He has put eternity in their hearts." Humanity was created with a natural desire to live forever. However, throughout the course of history mankind has looked in all the wrong places. Even today, there are some Christians looking in the wrong direction.

We must know in what manner Jesus will return.

To begin with, we will look at a descriptive passage in 1 Corinthians 15:51–54, the Bible promises, "Behold, I tell you a mystery: We shall not all sleep, but we shall all be changed—in a moment, in the twinkling of an eye, at the last trumpet. For the trumpet will sound, and the dead will be raised incorruptible, and we shall be changed. For this corruptible must put on incorruption, and this mortal must put on immortality. So when this corruptible has put on incorruption, and this mortal has put on immortality, then shall be brought to pass the saying that is written: 'Death is swallowed up in victory.' "

This passage says that the *corruptible* will put on incorruption. Literally in the original Greek, that word means perishable. We use this word often in the context of food—perishable and nonperishable food. Perishable food is that food which can spoil easily, nonperishable foods are those foods that are canned and packaged and will seemingly last forever. Right now, you and I are perishable goods. It may be a bit of a morbid thought, but as soon as we are born, we begin to die—because we are perishable. This corruptible, this mortal, will at that time put on incorruption and put on immortality. That immortality which from ancient times, civilizations have been striving to achieve, will be ours. Jesus is coming again to set up a kingdom of imperishable goods. He created us originally to last forever, but because of sin, we are bound by sin's consequence of death. But Jesus died to free us from that consequence and when He comes again that will be fully realized in His kingdom and His people which will last forever.

After that twinkling of an eye, after that last trumpet, after we have put on immortality, then what? We will get to see for ourselves what Jesus really meant when He said in John 14:2, 3, "In My Father's house are many mansions; if it were not so, I would have told you. I go to prepare a place for you. And if I go and prepare a place for you, I will come again and receive you to Myself; that where I am, there you may be also."

Jesus has prepared a wonderful place for us, described by the apostle John in Revelation 21:18–21, "The construction of its wall was of jasper; and the city was pure gold, like clear glass." And then John tells us that there are twelve foundations of the city and each of them made up of a different type of precious stone. He goes on to say, "The twelve gates were twelve pearls: each individual gate was of one pearl. And the street of the city was pure gold, like transparent glass." It will be a place of unparalleled beauty. This city and its inhabitants will last forever.

God has revealed this thrilling end-time plan in His Word and He wants us to be watching in the right direction. He doesn't want us to miss this beautiful and peaceful place.

Jesus desires that we would see with clear eyes and not be deceived. Let's go to the Bible with the eyes of our hearts and our minds open and discover how this will take place. How then will Christ return and take us to that most magnificent city described in Revelation 21?

First, it will be a literal event.

Luke 17:24 describes Jesus' coming, "For as the lightning that flashes out of one part under heaven shines to the other part under heaven, so also the Son of Man will be in His day." Here Jesus uses lightning to describe His coming. Lightning is real, it flashes and it streaks across the sky and people see it. It can be so bright that you can see it even with your eyes closed.

In the book of Acts, the Second Coming is described in a bit more detail. Acts 1:9–11 says, "Now when He [speaking of Jesus] had spoken these things, while they watched, He was taken up, and a cloud received Him out of their sight. And while they looked steadfastly toward heaven as He went up, behold, two men stood by them in white apparel, who also said, 'Men of Galilee, why do you stand gazing up into heaven? This same Jesus, who was taken up from you into heaven, will so come in like manner as you saw Him go into heaven.' " Jesus did not vanish from them, but he ascended to heaven. The disciples saw Him with their eyes. Then two heavenly beings taught them that the second coming of Jesus will resemble His ascension to heaven. A real Jesus ascended to heaven and a real Jesus Christ will descend at His second coming. Some have talked of Jesus' second coming merely being a spiritual coming. The Bible teaches that a real Jesus literally ascended up into heaven and that a real Jesus will literally descend from heaven through the atmosphere to this very planet we call home.

Just as Jesus' coming will be a literal event, it will also be a visible event

John described this visible event in Revelation 1:7, "Behold, He is coming with clouds, and every eye will see Him." The passage clearly states that every eye will see Him. His coming will not just be seen by believers, but all the inhabitants of the earth will observe His coming.

Jesus Himself said in Matthew 24:30, "Then the sign of the Son of Man will appear in heaven, and then all the tribes of the earth will mourn, and they will see the Son of Man coming on the clouds of heaven with power and great glory." All the tribes of the earth is a description of the entire population.

Everyone will see the coming of Jesus because it is a literal and visible event.

His coming will also be an audible event.

The apostle Paul outlined the second coming of Jesus in his first letter to the Thessalonians in chapter 4, verses 16, 17, "For the Lord Himself will descend from heaven with a shout, with the voice of an archangel, and with the trumpet of God. And the dead in Christ will rise first. Then we who are alive and remain shall be caught up together with them in the clouds to meet the Lord in the air. And thus we shall always be with the Lord." Paul here continues the theme of a literal and visible event, but he supplies the addition of an audible event. The voice of the archangel and the trumpet of God are not silent mediums of sound. This sound will reverberate all through the earth.

The first passage we looked at in this chapter, in 1 Corinthians 15:52 also emphasizes the audible nature of Christ's return, "in a moment, in the twinkling of an eye, at the last trumpet. For the trumpet will sound, and the dead will be raised incorruptible, and we shall be changed." God's trumpet will sound. I don't think that can be any kind of silent trumpet. That mighty sound will raise the dead from their sleep and slumber.

Christ's coming will be a literal event, it will be a visible event and it will be an audible event. *And His coming will most certainly be a glorious event*

Matthew 16:27, "For the Son of Man will come in the glory of His Father with His angels, and then He will reward each according to his works." In Revelation 19:11–14, Jesus is described in His glorious appearance, "Now I saw heaven opened, and behold, a white horse. And He who sat on him was called Faithful and True, and in righteousness He judges and makes war. His eyes were like a flame of fire, and on His head were many crowns. He had a name written that no one knew except Himself. He was clothed with a robe dipped in blood, and His name is called The Word of God. And the armies in heaven, clothed in fine linen, white and clean, followed Him on white horses."

There is a real Christ coming in the sky and a real Christ coming to resurrect the dead. It will be a glorious event.

Have you lost loved ones? Have you lost your parents? Maybe a spouse? A son or a daughter? Maybe a little baby? Jesus is literally, visibly, and audibly coming in glory to reunite you with those loved ones that put their trust and hope in Jesus. Why not put your trust fully in Him today?

Jesus second coming will also be a climactic event

Jesus promises to us in Revelation 22:12, "And behold, I am coming quickly, and My reward is with Me, to give to every one according to his work. I am the Alpha and the Omega, the Beginning and the End, the First and the Last." The second coming rewards each individual for the life they lived. It is the climax of human history. Some groups will be thrilled by His return, but others will not.

Revelation 6:15–17 gives vivid details of that day, "And the kings of the earth, the great men, the rich men, the commanders, the mighty men, every slave and every free man, hid themselves in the caves and in the rocks of the mountains, and said to the mountains and rocks, 'Fall on us and hide us from the face of Him who sits on the throne and from the wrath of the Lamb! For the great day of His wrath has come, and who is able to stand?' "

Who is able to stand? No one need be a part of the group that trembles at the coming of Christ. Jesus has made the provision for us to be able to stand. 2 Corinthians 1:24, tells us for "by faith you stand." We stand by faith, faith in what? Ephesians 2:8, 9 gives us the answer, "For by grace you have been saved through faith, and that not of yourselves; it is the gift of God, not of works, lest anyone should boast." We are able to stand, by faith in the grace of Christ. We must stop trusting in ourselves and trust fully in Jesus, He has made a way for us. Jesus is on our side, He is not out to get us, He wants to receive us.

Jesus is coming to take us to be with Him. And when He comes, it will be literal, it will be visible, it will be audible, it will be glorious and it will be climactic.

What about the secret rapture?

Some have said that the Bible depicts Jesus' coming as a thief, in secret. Citing Matthew 24:36, "But of that day and hour no one knows, not even the angels of heaven, but My Father only." Then also, verse 43, "But know this, that if the master of the house had known what hour the thief would come, he would have watched and not allowed his house to be broken into."

However, these texts do not seem to be describing a secretive manner. These texts are referring to time as is evidenced by the usage of the words *day* and *hour*. The timing of Jesus' return will be a secret but not the way in which He comes. Matthew 24:44 adds clarification when it says, "Therefore you also be ready, for the Son of Man is coming at an hour you do not expect." Clearly this is a reference to timing, not manner.

Please notice another reference to Jesus' coming as a thief in 2 Peter 3:10, "But the day of the Lord will come as a thief in the night, in which the heavens will pass away with a great noise, and the elements will melt with fervent heat; both the earth and the works that are in it will be burned up." Did you read that? In the same verse that describes Jesus' coming as a thief the same context uses great noise and fire, both audible and visible attributes. The Second Coming is a surprise for those that are unprepared.

Often those who believe in the secret rapture teach that the church will be raptured or removed before the tribulation. However, Revelation 16:15, again describes Jesus' second coming as a thief after the first six plagues or tribulation, "Behold, I am coming as a thief. Blessed is he who watches, and keeps his garments, lest he walk naked and they see his shame." Jesus' coming as a thief surprises those who have not daily prepared for that day.

What about the expression "one taken and the other left?"

Let's look at the passage, in Luke 17:36, "Two men will be in the field: the one will be taken and the other left."

But let's remember the context. In just a few verses previous, Jesus said in Luke 17:26, 28, "And as it was in the days of Noah, so it will be also in the days of the Son of Man: Likewise as it was also in the days of Lot: They ate, they drank, they bought, they sold, they planted, they built." Was the flood of Noah's day a secret? How about the destruction of Sodom and Gomorrah? No, each of these communities was thoroughly warned and the events were literal, visible, audible and climactic in nature. The issue of one taken and one left lets us know that before the coming of Jesus there will only be two classes of people, one saved and one lost. There is no additional chance. Right now we are living in our time to decide.

There is no second opportunity; the time to get serious is now. Paul admonishes us, in 2 Corinthians 6:2, "Behold, now is the accepted time; behold, now is the day of salvation."

Our eternal destiny is being settled by the choices we make today. Christ's coming will be a literal event, a visible event, an audible event, a glorious event, and a climactic event.

Equally important, the second coming of Jesus will be a joyous event.

Paul encourages us in Titus 2:13 to be "looking for the blessed hope and glorious appearing of our great God and Savior Jesus Christ."

The second coming of Jesus is the only real hope we have in this hopeless and helpless world. His second coming will make us new. It will reunite us with long-lost family members, and we will be able to cry out the words of Isaiah 25:9,

> And it will be said in that day:
> "Behold, this is our God;
> We have waited for Him, and He will save us.
> This is the LORD; We have waited for Him;
> We will be glad and rejoice in His salvation."

Jesus desires you as a friend. He wants you to be in His kingdom. He is coming again to take you home. He has made every provision for you to be there. He wants you to be there. He has given us signs of His return and He has told us how He will return. Today, won't you commit your life to Him.

Jesus is calling for you to come to Him. In Zechariah 1:3 the Lord says, "Return to Me," . . . "and I will return to you." You haven't gone too far. Jesus will accept you wherever you are.

He is coming again and He brings hope for the future, but He also brings hope for today. Do you desire that hope? Do you want to be filled with that hope? Let's pray and ask the Lord to give us hope.

Staying Wide Awake

"Watch therefore, for you do not know what hour your Lord is coming."
—*Matthew 24:42*

Have you ever anticipated something, then, because of a delay, you became distracted and lost your readiness?

During my childhood, camping was always the highlight of our summer. When the day for us to leave for our camping trip arrived, I would be up early and ready to go. But then the wait would begin. My mom put the finishing touches on getting the camper loaded, then we had to wait for my dad to come home from work.

I remember one particular occasion when we were going to Copper Harbor Michigan. I was ready to leave early that morning and kept asking my mom—is it time to go yet? But as the day wore on, I got distracted. I started playing with toys, no longer as anxious as before. Then before I knew it, it was time to go, but *then I was the one who wasn't ready*. I had toys to put away.

Could it be that many of us have drifted in our commitment to be ready for Jesus' return?

In Matthew 24:42–44, Jesus said these words, "Watch therefore, for you do not know what hour your Lord is coming. But know this, that if the master of the house had known what hour the thief would come, he would have watched and not allowed his house to be broken into. Therefore you also be ready, for the Son of Man is coming at an hour you do not expect."

Notice those two keys—watch and be ready.

In Matthew 24 Jesus gave signs of His return—this is what we are to watch for. But in Matthew 25, Jesus gave a series of three parables; the point of which is we need to be ready. In this chapter, we will study the first of those three parables. Let's read it in Matthew 25:1–13:

> "Then the kingdom of heaven shall be likened to ten virgins who took their lamps and went out to meet the bridegroom. Now five of them were wise, and five were foolish. Those who were foolish took their lamps and took no oil with them, but the wise took oil in their vessels with their lamps. But while the bridegroom was delayed, they all slumbered and slept.
>
> "And at midnight a cry was heard: 'Behold, the bridegroom is coming; go out to meet him!' Then all those virgins arose and trimmed their lamps. And the foolish said to the wise, 'Give us some of your oil, for our lamps are going out.' But the wise answered, saying, 'No, lest there should not be enough for us and you; but go rather to those who sell, and buy for yourselves.' And while they went to buy, the bridegroom came, and those who were ready went in with him to the wedding; and the door was shut.
>
> "Afterward the other virgins came also, saying, 'Lord, Lord, open to us!' But he answered and said,

'Assuredly, I say to you, I do not know you.' Watch therefore, for you know neither the day nor the hour in which the Son of Man is coming."

As we look at the text, Jesus begins in verse 1 by saying, "Then the kingdom of heaven shall be likened to ten virgins who took their lamps and went out to meet the bridegroom."

Jesus likens the kingdom of heaven to ten virgins, or bridesmaids, if you are looking at a different translation.

In this first verse, Jesus points out the three important elements of this parable: the ten virgins, their lamps, and the bridegroom. And we see that Jesus used imagery that was familiar to His disciples—the Eastern custom of a wedding. In that custom, the groom or bridegroom would go forth from his house with some of the wedding party. Along the way they would pick up various participants in the wedding, and finally they would arrive at the father of the bride's home. It is here where he would pick up his bride and then return to his home for a wedding feast.

- In the parable, the ten virgins are all a part of the wedding party and are awaiting the bridegroom.
- Christ is represented as the bridegroom, in this parable.
- The people He comes for are represented by the virgins—we are those virgins.
- Why does the parable call them virgins?
  ○ A virgin is pure and in this parable this represents a faith that is pure and unadulterated.
  ○ Each of them has a lamp, no doubt this is a reference to the Word of God. In Psalm 119:105 the Bible says, "Your word is a lamp to my feet

And a light to my path."

These ten virgins are awaiting the coming bridegroom and at first glance the ten virgins seem to be equal, but in verse 2 the text reveals a different story. "Now five of them were wise, and five were foolish. Those who were foolish took their lamps and took no oil with them, but the wise took oil in their vessels with their lamps. But while the bridegroom was delayed, they all slumbered and slept."

Jesus now divides these ten virgins into two classes. Five were wise and five were foolish. In the original the word *wise* literally means intelligent, prudent, sensible, and mindful of one's interests. And the word *foolish* in the original, means to be full of folly, impious, godless, and stupid.

Jesus divides the group in two, those that are wise, intelligent, and prudent and those that are foolish, full of folly, and impious. Verse 3 reveals the key characteristic of the foolish—they take no oil with them, while the wise carry extra oil with them. Why is this distinction important?

In that time, a lamp resembled a bowl, with the brim pinched at one point to make a spout. Into that spout a wick was inserted that would draw up the olive to fuel the flame. Lamps were kept burning day and night in ancient times, for the lamps served not only to give light but also to keep fire at hand.

The lamp of Jesus' time would be comparable to today's flashlight. Just like a lamp needed oil, a flashlight needs batteries. And in Jesus' time if you didn't have any oil, you didn't have any light.

Throughout Scripture oil, especially olive oil, is used symbolically as a symbol for the Holy Spirit. Here in this parable, Jesus has made it very clear that all ten virgins have a pure faith and each of them has the lamp of the Word of God, but only five of them have the fuel of the Holy Spirit.

Clearly, having a head knowledge of the Word of God is not enough. In this parable, Jesus teaches that a head knowledge of the Word without the oil of the Holy Spirit is just foolishness and folly. However, this story reveals that despite their differences these two groups resemble each other more than one might think. The Bible states that the bridegroom was delayed and then all of them slumbered and slept. Both the wise and foolish slumbered—becoming careless and drowsy, and nodding off. Then they slept. The word for *slept* is the same word used to refer to *death*. This was a deep sleep. They were no longer watching, they were no longer ready, they were no longer paying attention, they were sleeping as if they were dead.

Are you struggling today in your relationship with Jesus? Does it seem to you that your religious experience is almost dead? There is hope. Listen to the remainder of this parable:

> "And at midnight a cry was heard: 'Behold, the bridegroom is coming; go out to meet him!' Then all those virgins arose and trimmed their lamps. And the foolish said to the wise, 'Give us some of your oil, for our lamps are going out.' But the wise answered, saying, 'No, lest there should not be enough for us and you; but go rather to those who sell, and buy for yourselves.' And while they went to buy, the bridegroom came, and those who were ready went in with him to the wedding; and the door was shut.
>
> "Afterward the other virgins came also, saying, 'Lord, Lord, open to us!' But he answered and said,

'Assuredly, I say to you, I do not know you' "
(Matthew 25:6–11).

In the original language, it literally says "in the middle of the night." At the deepest and darkest hour of the night a cry goes forth, *"The bridegroom is coming now; go out to meet him!"* I picture in my own mind the surprise of the virgins. Do you remember a time where you were startled out of a deep, slumbering sleep? These virgins are having that same experience. Bewildered and groggy they get up and trim their lamps. They took the burnt portions of the wick, cut it off, and then replenish their supply of oil.

At this point that the foolish realize that they have no oil and so they ask the wise for some of theirs. And this request is denied. This may seem selfish, but it emphasizes the point that we cannot be responsible for someone else's salvation nor can someone be responsible for ours. We can show someone to Christ, we can show them His ways and we can demonstrate what a living faith looks like, but each individual is responsible for their own salvation.

This is why Paul says in Philippians 2:12, "Work out your own salvation with fear and trembling." *Only we can take responsibility for our own salvation.* This is a key point of the passage—we, individually, must be ready for the return of Christ. *We must take responsibility for being ready.*

While this passage is direct counsel to those who claim to be God's people, the most troubling fact is that all ten fell asleep. I have to wonder how the end of the parable would have played out if the wise had stayed awake. They could have warned the foolish. This parable is a call for God's people to wake up.

The ending is very disappointing but abundantly clear.

There will be a time when it is too late to make a decision to follow Jesus. The foolish virgins had the knowledge of where to go to get the oil, but they did not utilize that knowledge until it was too late. And later, as they try to get into the banquet as late arrivals, they hear the most disappointing words anyone could ever hear. Jesus, the Bridegroom, says to them—I never knew you. *Time will eventually run out for people to make a decision and there is no second chance for that decision.*

The last verse of this passage gives us our last point, "Watch therefore, for you know neither the day nor the hour in which the Son of Man is coming" (Matthew 25:13).

This passage advises us to be spiritually awake and to be in a state of constant readiness. The only difference between the foolish and the wise is that the wise have an intent desire to do all that is within their power to be ready for the coming of the bridegroom. And because of that they find themselves receiving the reward of the promise. *Preparedness is the key.* This parable outlines how we are to be ready for the return of Jesus. It gives us hope in the midst of this helpless and hopeless planet.

It calls upon us to use that lamp—the Word of God—and to be daily filled with the Holy Spirit. Taking personal responsibility for our spiritual life. It's time to wake up. We need to stop just going through the motions. We must wake up and get our spiritual house in order. We must realize that time will eventually run out. We need to wake up now and stay awake. Is that your desire today? Do you want to have a living relationship with Jesus and be in a constant state of readiness for His return?

He is coming to take those who are ready home. Do you want to be ready?

Jesus says in John 6:37, "The one who comes to Me I

will by no means cast out." Jesus doesn't reject anyone who comes to Him. Today let's come to Jesus and commit to a life of reading the Scripture, being filled with the Holy Spirit, and being ready to meet Him.

Dear Father in heaven, we come to You today. We are sorry that, like those ten virgins, we have slept and slumbered, but we want to be awake, we want to be ready. Today Lord give us the strength to leave everything else and focus completely on You. We have been distracted. Today we come to Your Son, Jesus, who has promised that He won't turn us away. As we give our lives to Him, help us to be ready for His soon return. We pray in Jesus' name, Amen.

Who's Got Talent?

"Well done, good and faithful servant;
you have been faithful over a few things,
I will make you ruler over many things."
—Matthew 25:23

A Northern California couple by the name of John and Mary were on their daily walk with their dog—the same route they had walked for many years. As they walked along their property they noticed something sticking out of the ground. It looked like a rusty can, but they weren't sure. They hadn't noticed it before, but that day they saw it, and it intrigued them. They began to dig around the object and eventually unearthed eight rusty cans. While that may not seem like much of a find, the contents of those metal cans was truly amazing.

They found a cache of fourteen hundred rare nineteenth-century coins, and it is estimated to be worth more than ten million US dollars. Their find might well be the greatest buried treasure ever found in the United States! No one knows exactly how they got there. Some thought it was money from a bank robbery. However, that theory has been proven false. It seems that someone buried the coins and died before they let anyone know where they were.

Is it possible that we are sitting on a buried treasure?

Could it be that this "pot of gold" could teach us a lesson in how we might be ready for the return of Jesus?

In Matthew 25 there are three parables. Each of these parables demonstrates the answer to Jesus' call to watch and be ready from Matthew 24. In this chapter, we look at the second of those parables. Matthew 25:14 reads, "For the kingdom of heaven is like a man traveling to a far country, who called his own servants and delivered his goods to them." In the Greek, the word used, instead of the phrase "the kingdom of heaven," is *it*. By using the word *it*, Jesus draws us back to the previous parable. There Jesus talks about the kingdom of God through the story of the ten virgins, reminding us about the importance of our personal readiness and accountability. All three parables in Matthew 25 are connected to Jesus' words of Matthew 24. This is not just a series of individual stories strung together. Jesus wants us to clearly understand the factors that relate to our being ready for His return.

As we look at this parable—and remember these are stories that are metaphorical or symbolic in nature—in this one the master going on a journey is representative of Jesus Christ and is a reference to His departure and soon return. Verse 15 reads, "And to one he gave five talents, to another, two, and to another, one, each according to his own ability; and he went on his journey."

As we analyze what this parable is saying, we must look deeper into some of the words, so we might better understand. The word "ability" is the Greek word *dunamis*. It means strength or power. In the King James Version, it is often translated as "mighty works." However, when *dunamis* is used it is often in association with God's power and His strength, especially the power of the Holy Spirit. This gives us the sense that although these servants have been given according to their personal ability, these abilities are themselves God-given attributes.

The master gave them talents, according to their ability. The talent in New Testament times was both a weight of measure and a coin. Here in this parable, as we will read in just a moment, there is no question that it is referring to the coin. And just to help us in our understanding of the parable, the value of such coin in today's money would be worth approximately forty-seven hundred dollars. However, our concern should be the value of a talent in New Testament times. Please follow me as we do just a little math. What is the daily wage in the New Testament? In Matthew 20:2 it talks about a day's wage being one penny or denarius. The talent, in New Testament times, was worth about six thousand denarii. If we figure three hundred working days per year, that means that the slave who received only one talent received almost twenty years' worth of wages. The one who received two equaled almost forty years' worth of wages and the one who received five, almost one hundred years' worth of wages. This was no small sum of money! *Just one talent was a significant value.*

As we journey through this parable, we will see that the talent is symbolic of the skills and abilities God has given us to grow His kingdom. After giving each of the servants their talents, the master leaves for a journey.

As we begin this passage it is clear that *everyone is given some gift or skill in accordance with his ability—which was given by God for expanding His kingdom.* Let's get further into the parable, "Then he who had received the five talents went and traded with them, and made another five talents. And likewise he who had received two gained two more also.

But he who had received one went and dug in the ground, and hid his lord's money" (Matthew 25:16–18).

Unmistakably, there is an expectation that we are to utilize the gift or gifts given to us by God.

In verse 16 it simply says, "then." In more modern versions it says, "immediately." The Greek literally says that he went without delay. The one who received the five talents immediately utilized those gifts and the passage says the one with two did likewise. The passage also says, "he traded" with them. Quite literally it means he invested them, or made them work for him.

Although the text does not plainly state instructions from the master, these first two servants knew that these talents were to be put to use. They were to be taken to the marketplace and profited on. However, the third slave does something very interesting—he digs a hole and hides the money in the ground. He does nothing with his talent.

Eventually the master returns to settle accounts. The King James Version says he "reckoneth"—the master came to see how they used what he had given them. Continuing on in verses 19–23,

"After a long time the lord of those servants came and settled accounts with them.

"So he who had received five talents came and brought five other talents, saying, 'Lord, you delivered to me five talents; look, I have gained five more talents besides them.' His lord said to him, 'Well done, good and faithful servant; you were faithful over a few things, I will make you ruler over many things. Enter into the joy of your lord.' He also who had received two talents came and said, 'Lord, you delivered to me two talents; look, I have gained two more talents besides them.' His lord said to him, 'Well done, good and faithful servant; you have been faithful over a few things, I will make you ruler over many things. Enter into the joy of your lord.' "

But verses 24–30 tell us about the servant who received one talent,

"Then he who had received the one talent came and said, 'Lord, I knew you to be a hard man, reaping where you have not sown, and gathering where you have not scattered seed. And I was afraid, and went away and hid your talent in the ground. Look, there you have what is yours.'

"But his lord answered and said to him, 'You wicked and lazy servant, you knew that I reap where I have not sown, and gather where I have not scattered seed. So you ought to have deposited my money with the bankers, and at my coming I would have received back my own with interest. Therefore take the talent from him, and give it to him who has ten talents.

" 'For to everyone who has, more will be given, and he will have abundance; but from him who does not have, even what he has will be taken away. And cast the unprofitable servant into the outer darkness. There will be weeping and gnashing of teeth.' "

Part of God's judgment will be based upon how we utilized our gifts. But the promise of hope is that the joy of the Lord awaits those who obey and use their gifts.

God has placed us to be a beacon of hope on this dark planet. He's given us each gifts. Maybe its money—how are we blessing the world around us with this gift from God? Maybe He's given the ability to cook or bake, how are we using that ability given by God? How about something as simple as time—what are we doing with our time to bless those around us?

Jesus has a wonderful place of hope prepared for us. He wants you to be there, but He also desires those around you to be there. How are you using the gifts, talents and abilities to prepare those around you for the second coming of Jesus?

Today, do you want to offer your life to Jesus? Do you want to offer your life for His glory and to expand His kingdom? Do you want to be used as a tool to bring hope to this helpless and hopeless planet?

The Accountability Factor

"Assuredly, I say to you, inasmuch as you did it to one of the least of these My brethren, you did it to Me."
—Matthew 25:40

Have you ever wondered what the difference between a sheep and goat is? I'm not farmer, and I need to be careful in analyzing animals that I have not worked with. However, a little research yields some noted differences. For example, goats are considered browsers, they nibble at their food, which is usually leaves, tender shoots, or other soft vegetation; often only eating the tips. Sheep, on the other hand, are grazers who feed for hours at a time, eating small portions of food all day long. They love clover and grasses and eat it right down to the soil. Goats are naturally curious creatures and very independent; sheep, like to stay in the flock. In fact, when a sheep is away from the flock, they become agitated and upset.

One other difference is that most goats have hair while sheep have wool. These are just a few of the differences, but why all of this talk about sheep and goats?

We have been studying about hope for a helpless planet. We have looked at Jesus' reminder and warning in Matthew

24 to watch and be ready. And in Matthew 25 we now look at the third in a series of three parables that teach us how to be ready for the return of Jesus. Listen to these words of Jesus in Matthew 25:31–33, "When the Son of Man comes in His glory, and all the holy angels with Him, then He will sit on the throne of His glory. All the nations will be gathered before Him, and He will separate them one from another, as a shepherd divides his sheep from the goats. And He will set the sheep on His right hand, but the goats on the left."

This parable uses metaphorical or symbolic language to describe the judgment. How will Jesus decide who is and who is not going to heaven. He makes the comparison to sheep and goats. The sheep He places on His right hand, but the goats on His left. Right at the outset, before any information is given, we see a difference. In the Bible, the right hand is a symbol of power or favor. The sheep seem to be favored for some reason, but why?

Jesus gives the answer in verses 34–36, "Then the King will say to those on His right hand, 'Come, you blessed of My Father, inherit the kingdom prepared for you from the foundation of the world: for I was hungry and you gave Me food; I was thirsty and you gave Me drink; I was a stranger and you took Me in; 'I was naked and you clothed Me; I was sick and you visited Me; I was in prison and you came to Me.'"

Wow, did you hear that? We have had several studies on the joy of going to heaven. These sheep, which represent God's true people, are invited into the courts of heaven.

Sheep are often used to describe God's people in the Bible. In John 10:4, Jesus uses the illustration, "And when he brings out his own sheep, he goes before them; and the sheep follow him, for they know his voice." Sheep know the voice of the shepherd, the Shepherd is Jesus. Because the sheep follow His example, they feed the hungry, they provide drink to the thirsty, they provide shelter to the homeless, clothing for the naked, and comfort and healing for the sick. Do you see what is happening here? Jesus is inviting those individuals into heaven who have provided acts of kindness.

Right now, I know what someone is thinking, *Are you saying that people are saved by their works?* No not at all. I fully believe the words of Ephesians 2:8, 9, "For by grace you have been saved through faith, and that not of yourselves; it is the gift of God, not of works, lest anyone should boast."

I also believe Titus 3:5: "Not by works of righteousness which we have done, but according to His mercy He saved us, through the washing of regeneration and renewing of the Holy Spirit." Those who will go to heaven are saved by the grace and mercy of God alone.

I want you to notice something very interesting though, while we are not saved by our works, listen to these words in Revelation 20:13, "And they were judged, each one according to his works." That seems a little confusing, and I don't want to confuse you more but listen to the very words of Jesus in Matthew 16:27, "For the Son of Man will come in the glory of His Father with His angels, and then He will reward each according to his works." Now here is the principle, *we are saved 100 percent by the grace and mercy of God*—it is His gift to us as we make a decision to follow Him—*but we are judged by our works.*

How does that work? As Jesus enters our life and saves a sinner like me—who doesn't deserve His salvation—His grace and mercy makes me worthy. Jesus makes my imperfect heart and life perfect. He invites me to come as I am, but He doesn't want me to stay that way. He invites me and gives me the power to change. As we make a decision to follow Jesus, He cleanses us and takes away our sin and the Holy Spirit enters our life and begins to change us. How so? In Galatians 5:22–25 it tells us, "But the fruit of the Spirit is love, joy, peace, longsuffering, kindness, goodness, faithfulness, gentleness, self-control. Against such there is no law. And those who are Christ's have crucified the flesh with its passions and desires. If we live in the Spirit, let us also walk in the Spirit."

As we walk with Jesus and give our life to Him, the Holy Spirit produces the fruit of the Spirit in our lives. This is why Jesus says in Matthew 7:20, "Therefore by their fruits you will know them." Several years ago I learned the art of grafting trees, specifically apple trees. During that time I have tried close to one hundred different varieties of apples. And, if I go into an orchard, I am pretty good at identifying what is an apple tree and what is a peach tree. But I really wouldn't know with absolute certainty until those trees produced fruit. And here lies the principle of the Christian life; the fruit we bear demonstrates who we are. This is why the Bible can say we are saved by the grace of God, but judged by our works. This is why Solomon wrote the words of Ecclesiastes 12:14, "For God will bring every work into judgment, Including every secret thing, Whether good or evil." Our works or our actions speak to who we really are. What is that old saying? "Actions speak louder than words." Which is why Jesus further emphasized in John 5:29, "and come forth—those who have done good, to the resurrection of life, and those who have done evil, to the resurrection of condemnation." The sheep in this parable have done good. But remember our doing good isn't putting together some kind of checklist of good deeds where I try and try to accumulate enough good deeds to offset the bad deeds. No, we are saved by grace and as the grace of Jesus works in us, it changes us into a person who naturally does acts of kindness, because it is the fruit we bear.

These acts of kindness become unconscious actions, Matthew continues in Matthew 25:37–40, "Then the righteous will answer Him, saying, 'Lord, when did we see You hungry and feed You, or thirsty and give You drink? When did we see You a stranger and take You in, or naked and clothe You? Or when did we see You sick, or in prison, and come to You?' And the King will answer and say to them, 'Assuredly, I say to you, inasmuch as you did it to one of the least of these My brethren, you did it to Me.' " What a beautiful message of hope—those who are being transformed into the likeness of Jesus do the works of Jesus and now He invites them home to be with him eternally!

We could stop the teaching right here, but friend, it wouldn't be complete. There is another group, those on the left, those who are referred to as goats. Their story isn't as bright and, is in fact, very sad. The words of Jesus are almost painful to read, listen in verses 41–46,

> "Then He will also say to those on the left hand, 'Depart from Me, you cursed, into the everlasting fire prepared for the devil and his angels: for I was hungry and you gave Me no food; I was thirsty and you gave Me no drink; I was a stranger and you did not take Me in, naked and you did not clothe Me, sick and in prison and you did not visit Me.'

> "Then they also will answer Him, saying, 'Lord, when did we see You hungry or thirsty or a stranger or naked or sick or in prison, and did not minister

to You?' Then He will answer them, saying, 'Assuredly, I say to you, inasmuch as you did not do it to one of the least of these, you did not do it to Me.' And these will go away into everlasting punishment, but the righteous into eternal life."

Those on the left hand are judged by the same principle—their works. But this group has neglected the hungry, ignored the thirsty, shunned the homeless, overlooked the naked, and disregarded the sick. They were oblivious to the needs in their community around them. They didn't have a life-giving relationship with Jesus. These are those that are self-centered; they sense no need of Jesus and thus don't bear good fruit.

But I want you to notice that *the lost, don't have to be lost.* See there in verse 41 and 46 it describes the destination of those who won't go to heaven, it calls it "the everlasting fire prepared for the devil and his angels" or "everlasting punishment." This word "everlasting" describes the permanence of their situation and that it can't be undone. But did you notice that hell is prepared for a very specific group—the devil and his angels. Hell was and is never intended for human beings, so what happened?

In life we have two choices, to follow Jesus or to follow our own way. Our own way is ultimately choosing the way of Satan—rebellion. The final destruction of hellfire was not prepared for humans, but humans who choose to cling to their sin will be destroyed with their sin, which is destroyed with the devil.

How sad! The reason this is a tragedy, is that it doesn't have to be this way. Jesus stretches out His arms and says, "Come to Me, come and I will offer you eternal life." But there seems to be a whole group that is familiar with a theory of religion, but the gospel has affected no change in their lives—there is no fruit. Jesus cries out for us to accept His life-changing gift of salvation.

Romans 10:13 makes this promise, "Whoever calls on the name of the LORD shall be saved." When Jesus calls us, He invites us to come as we are—then He changes us that we might bear beautiful fruit.

Jesus does wonderful work for us and in us. Then that mighty saving power will stir in us dramatic change, and the Holy Spirit will work in us so that we might produce an abundance of good fruit—the good works that Jesus mentions in the parable.

Maybe this year you're thinking about going and buying a fruit tree for your back yard. Maybe you're going to buy an apple tree. The tag says it's an apple tree, it looks like an apple tree and in fact you believe it is an apple tree. But here is the reality: you won't really know that it is an apple tree until it produces fruit.

In the same way, we can profess to being a Christian, we can attend church, we can even look the part, but what does our fruit say about us? It's time. Jesus is coming soon. And He is saying watch and be ready. Part of getting ready is to have a real living faith that is active and producing good fruit. The fruit we bear doesn't save us; it clarifies who we are and whom we serve. Can you imagine, what would happen in our communities if each of us took the charge of Jesus seriously? Could you imagine what might happen in the large cities, the small cities, the villages, and communities? What might happen if every believer in Christ felt compelled to look around in his or her communities and provide for the needs that exist there?

Friend, do you sense Jesus calling you today? Do you sense Jesus appealing for you to enter into a serious and committed relationship with Him today? Maybe you feel overwhelmed because you think you are just too far away. Jesus calls and says, " 'Not by might nor by power, but by My Spirit' says the LORD" (Zechariah 4:6). We can't change ourselves by simply digging our heels in and trying harder. But we can give our life to Jesus, and He changes us.

Do you want to invite Jesus into your heart today? Do you want to recommit yourself to Him today? Do you want to clasp His hand in faith and say, "Jesus save me and make me a fruit bearer so I am prepared for your kingdom?"

Oh Father in heaven, we know we fall far short of the standard that You have set up. We need You, we want to reflect You. We want people to see Your Son, Jesus, in us. Today we give our hearts and lives to You. Please change us into Your likeness. We pray in Jesus' name. Amen.

The Final Journey

"Behold, the tabernacle of God is with men, and He will dwell with them, and they shall be His people. God Himself will be with them and be their God."

—*Revelation 21:3*

Howard Carter, an English archaeologist, searched Egypt for a seemingly impossible discovery—the tomb of the young king, Tutankhamen. After searching for this lost tomb for many years, Carter followed a lead in 1922 that he hoped would bring success—and it did! He contacted the financier of the expedition, Lord Carnarvon and waited for his arrival. Upon Carnarvon's arrival, he and Carter descended the steps of the site in the Valley of the Kings. Carter made a small breach in the entryway and peered in. Read his words he used to describe what he saw, "At first I could see nothing, the hot air escaping from the chamber causing the candle flame to flicker. But presently as my eyes grew accustomed to the lights, details of the room within emerged slowly from the midst. Strange animals, statues, and gold . . . everywhere the glitter of gold." Howard Carter was stunned. He continued, describing what happened next: "For a moment—an eternity it must have seemed to others standing by—I was struck dumb with amazement. And when Lord Carnarvon . . . inquired anxiously, 'Can you see anything?' it was all I could do to get out the words 'Yes, wonderful things.' "

Gold and statues—are these things wonderful? Can such things bring us any happiness or hope?

Do the riches of gold and precious stones offer hope for this helpless planet? No, our only hope is found in those precious words of Jesus in John 14:1–3, "Let not your heart be troubled; you believe in God, believe also in Me. In My Father's house are many mansions; if it were not so, I would have told you. I go to prepare a place for you. And if I go and prepare a place for you, I will come again and receive you to Myself; that where I am, there you may be also. And where I go you know, and the way you know."

The Bible also says in 1 Corinthians 2:9, "But as it is written: Eye has not seen, nor ear heard, nor have entered into the heart of man the things which God has prepared for those who love Him." Heaven is more than you could ever imagine. Take a moment; just think back to the happiest time in your life. Do you have that image in your mind? Heaven will outdo it every time.

The Bible tells us what we ought to be looking forward to in 2 Peter 3:13, "Nevertheless we, according to His promise, look for new heavens and a new earth in which righteousness dwells." The Bible says God's going to create a new heaven and a new earth. Revelation 21:1 reads, "Now I saw a new heaven and a new earth, for the first heaven and the first earth had passed away." It's not a make-believe place. It's not a fairy tale. It's a *real place* for *real people* to live forever with Jesus. Sin and suffering will be over. The sorrow and heartache of the past will be gone.

Down through the ages there have been men and women of faith who have looked forward to the coming of Jesus

Christ. They looked for the day when the sad drama of sin would be over and heaven would be their home. The Bible speaks of Abraham and his hope in Hebrews 11:10, "For he waited for the city which has foundations, whose builder and maker is God." Heaven is a real place, and God has made it for you and me. There are many things I do not know. But, I know for sure, that there's a better land coming. I know for sure, this world is not our home.

This world where terrorists board buses and kill innocent men, women, and children is not our home. This world where a teenager goes into his school and stabs twenty-two people is not our home. There must be something better. This world where a fourteen-year-old girl dies of leukemia is not our home.

This world is not our home. Doesn't your heart cry out for something better? God has a better plan. You were created for something better. Heaven is our home. Heaven is our hope.

Listen to the promise of scripture in Revelation 21:2–4 "Then I, John, saw the holy city, New Jerusalem, coming down out of heaven from God, prepared as a bride adorned for her husband. And I heard a loud voice from heaven saying, 'Behold, the tabernacle of God is with men, and He will dwell with them, and they shall be His people. God Himself will be with them and be their God. And God will wipe away every tear from their eyes; there shall be no more death, nor sorrow, nor crying. There shall be no more pain, for the former things have passed away.' "

Our home is with Him. He made us and He wants us to be with Him. He takes this earth that is hopeless and helpless and He makes it over again—no more death, sorrow, or crying. Don't you sense your heart longing to be there?

The Bible describes the heavenly city of Jerusalem where we'll live, in verse 12, 13, "Also she had a great and high wall with twelve gates, and twelve angels at the gates, and names written on them, which are the names of the twelve tribes of the children of Israel: three gates on the east, three gates on the north, three gates on the south, and three gates on the west." The gates are wide open for you. He's not trying to keep anyone out.

The names of the sons of Jacob, the tribes of Israel, are written there. Their stories show that they were liars, murderers and cheats—they would be convicted in any court of law. Their names are on the gates to testify that anyone who claims the grace of Jesus can walk through those gates. The sons of Jacob were sinners redeemed by the grace and mercy of God.

In verse 14 we read, "Now the wall of the city had twelve foundations, and on them were the names of the twelve apostles of the Lamb." The twelve apostles were imperfect men. Peter the denier; James and John, the sons of thunder. These names indicate that they were sinners saved by grace. *God wants us to know that if they can make it, so can we.*

You can enter through the gates of that city because it is your home by the grace of God. Maybe you feel unworthy—whatever you've done, His grace can forgive you. Whatever you've failed in, His grace can transform your life. He can make you into a new man. He can make you into a new woman.

The Bible even describes the measurements of the city in verse 16, "He measured the city with the reed: twelve thousand furlongs. Its length, breadth, and height are equal." A furlong is an old measurement of just over six hundred feet; so twelve thousand furlongs all the way around would be almost 350 miles per side! A mathematician once estimated that the New Jerusalem could house two billion people just on the ground floor. If magnificent, multistory buildings were used, the possibilities would be endless. There is room for you. There is room for me. He wants you there.

Paul, in Philippians 3:20, says, "For our citizenship is in heaven." Friends, our citizenship is not in any country of this world. Our citizenship is in heaven—a perfect place of perfect peace.

The Bible says of heaven in Isaiah 33:24 "And the inhabitant will not say, 'I am sick'; The people who dwell in it will be forgiven their iniquity." Can you imagine? No more cancer. No more heart disease. The Bible says we will not have sickness anymore. No more pain.

Isaiah 35:5, 6 goes on to describe this wonderful place,

Then the eyes of the blind shall be opened,
And the ears of the deaf shall be unstopped.
Then the lame shall leap like a deer,
And the tongue of the dumb sing.

The eyes of the blind are opened. The deaf will hear. Those with physical ailments will leap like deer and the person who cannot talk will speak. Can you imagine the excitement?

What rejoicing there will be that day! Rejoicing, running, leaping. Our bodies are filled with perfect vitality. In heaven new life and strength flow through our bodies. It is a new body with a new life. Heaven is our hope in this helpless world.

We read earlier that the Bible says, "And God will wipe away every tear from their eyes; there'll be no more death, nor sorrow, nor crying." Violence will be no more. War will be no more. The weapons of war will be put down. The Bible describes even more wonder of this place in Isaiah 65:17, 21–22,

> "For behold, I create new heavens and a new earth;
> And the former shall not be remembered or come to
>   mind. . . .
> They shall build houses and inhabit them;
> They shall plant vineyards and eat their fruit.
> They shall not build and another inhabit;
> They shall not plant and another eat."

We will have our city home in the New Jerusalem, which Jesus has built for us, but we will build our own homes in the county. It will be ours to live in, not built for someone else. We will grow lush gardens. You can build your dream home in the country. All the great minds of the ages who are committed Christians will help you design your dream home. And if necessary, the community of love and faith will help you to build it. The Bible says, "They shall build houses and inhabit them; they shall plant vineyards and eat their fruit."

Another amazing thing about heaven is fellowship and friends. Think of the great people of faith throughout history that we will be able to spend time with, Matthew 8:11 says, "And I say to you that many will come from east and west, and sit down with Abraham, Isaac, and Jacob in the kingdom of heaven." Imagine meeting Noah, Moses, John the Baptist, Peter, and John!

But above everything else in the beauty and perfection of heaven, we may sit down with Jesus face-to-face. There you meet the One who died for your sins. There you see the

One who has the eternal scars that serve as a reminder of His great sacrifice.

As you sit with Jesus, He talks about His love for us. He tells us how much we are worth. And He tells us that He died for us. He shares how He's been so anxious for us to be with Him in heaven. We sit at His feet and have never felt such love and acceptance.

The Bible says, Revelation 22:4, "They shall see His face, and His name shall be on their foreheads." They shall see His face. We fall at the feet of Jesus and with the angels and the redeemed we sing, "Worthy, worthy, worthy is the Lamb, who's been slain, for ever and ever and ever." We sing praises to His name.

Can you imagine the conversations that we have with Jesus that day? He says, "Do you see those flowers? I made them just for you." As we walk through fields of grain, Jesus picks some of the grain and says, "Taste it. I know your taste buds. I made that grain just for you. It's the only variety like it in the world. There is no other."

The flowers, the trees, the fruit, and everything else He shows you with His desire for it to be special for you. Can you picture it? I can imagine that we would have only one reaction—to fall at His feet and cry and say, "Jesus, all I want is You. I don't need the flowers in the field. I don't need the grain. Lord, all I need is You. Your love is enough for me. I don't need the mansion over there on the hill. That's a bonus. I don't need the gardens over there, that's a bonus. But, Jesus, all I want is You because Your love has filled every need in my heart."

It is in His presence in heaven that we find peace, joy, happiness and most of all . . . *hope*. The hope that He offers isn't just for the future; He offers that peace and hope today.

Do you sense the Spirit of God touching your heart? Maybe you've drifted away and now God is calling you. Don't hesitate; give your heart to Him today. What is stopping you from giving your heart to Jesus today, why not, say right now, "Jesus by Your grace, I will be in heaven for eternity?"

Maybe you need to take a bigger step than you've taken in the past; maybe you need to make a full commitment and be baptized as a public expression of your faith in Jesus. Maybe you need to say to Jesus that you're coming back today to stay with Him forever. Maybe you're facing a problem in your life, some habit that keeps you from following Jesus all the way. Maybe today, you want to say to Him that you are surrendering all to Him.

In the Lord's Presence there is hope. Hope for our future. Hope for all who live in this helpless and hopeless world. Jesus wants us to be in His presence. Do you want to accept His invitation today?

Father in heaven, thank You for Jesus. Thank You for His love. Thank You for His grace. Thank You for His mercy. Thank You for the hope You give us. Oh, Lord, we love You with all of our hearts. We want to be in heaven with You. Today, Father, move on our hearts as we commit ourselves to You. We look forward to being with You through all eternity. In Jesus' name, Amen.

Notes

Notes

Notes

Notes

Notes

Notes